RENAULT 5
'Le Car'

RENAULT 5
'Le Car'

David Sparrow

Acknowledgements

Published in 1992 by Osprey Publishing Ltd.
59 Grosvenor Street, London WIX 9DA

©David Sparrow 1992

ISBN 1-85532-230-7

Editor Shaun Barrington
Page design Angela Posen
Printed in Hong Kong

The photographs in this book were taken with the wonderful Leica R6 and M4-P. The lenses used vary from 16mm Fisheye to 560mm Long Focus, carried in a Billingham bag!

Lots of people have given freely of their time and expertise. Heartfelt thanks to you all.

Paula Batchelor at Renault Paris; Roger Ormisher at Renault UK; Lincoln Small, Peter Holmes, Ann Cosstick, Ian Anderson, and all the staff at Radbourne Racing in Wimbledon; Charley Carcreff at Automobile Scora for his amazing Maxi 5; Gerard Ward, for driving 5s around Normandy; Lydia Plant, at New Bedford College, for her kind assistance in making a fine location available; the staff and Directors of Chambord, for their kind and generous cooperation in allowing me to photograph Clio in their grounds; Graham Ellis, General Manager of Wimbledon Greyhound Stadium; Steve Loughlin of Formula Print and his Racing Mechanic David Borroff for allowing me to photograph their car during racing sessions.

Owners, Patricia Bartlet, Ursula Bartleet, David Murphy, Jason Church, Jaqueline Souras, Nicky McDougal, Alan Williamson. Models, Emma Prescott, Lara Leal, Gloria Fox, Amelia and Juliet Richardson.

Contents

Introduction

By the Twenties, French car makers were building large fast cars to transport the rich to the Côte D'Azur, Biarritz, and Deauville. It became the thing to do to motor out of Paris for the summer. The era of the 'Grand Touring' car had arrived. The war put a stop to it; private motoring would never be the same again.

After the war, the roads were bad, petrol was in short supply, and the need for cheap, reliable transport, capable of coping with those dreadful roads, was paramount. But something else had changed too. By the 1950s, the French motor industry had taken on board the proposition that women would buy cars. Renault launched the Dauphine, a car whose popularity with women became legendary. Throughout the 1960s the quality of life improved, and the state of the roads with it. For the fashion-conscious, the really frugal small car was either the appallingly slow Citroen 2Cv or the BMC Mini – not the sort of car to take from one end of France to the other – at least not with company and luggage.

Happily, Renault introduced the top-selling R4 in 1961. The R4 – or 4L, as it was also known – was a real friend to the Régie and to its millions of owners. 'Noddy', as it was also familiarly called, saved Renault's bacon when, in the early 1960s, production had dropped from 550,000 to 400,000 units and workers were calling lightning strikes.

This remarkably versatile car and its goods-carrying counterpart, the Fourgon, offered the answer for the stringency of the times.

Summoning his design team, Renault supremo Dreyfus said 'What I want you to come up with is a holdall on wheels – a travelling bag that can go anywhere without feeling self-conscious. It must be as tough as a rhino and cost a lot less to run. People will go to church in it, will go camping, will commute to the office, will make it a livestock carrier, a shop, a wedding car, a car for lovers ...'

It was significant, too, that the R4's design introduced the front-wheel-drive format that would equip almost all Renault models for the future, following the phasing out of the rear-engined cars.

Initially, the 4 had the 747cc motor of the classic Renault 4 CV but it hardly matched the versatility of the car, and first the 850 and then the 1100 units were offered, boosting the power considerably. Springing was by torsion bar and steering was by rack and pinion.

Factors that made the Renault 4 a winner were the four doors plus big tailgate, the excellent headroom and the wide adapt-

ability of the vehicle as a whole. 'Give me a holdall' was what Dreyfus had said, and that was what he and millions of customers got.

When the Régie introduced the Renault 6 in 1968, it had taken its first step towards the Renault 5, which may sound a numerical nonsense, but the firm have never felt bound to strict sequence in the numbers game.

The Renault 6 was a pretty little hatchback with an engine capacity option of 850 or 1100cc. Some people regarded it as a more elegant version of R4, but others saw it as a scaled-down version of the big R16 which had become a best seller in the upper sector of the market. Actually it was a less sophisticated form of the R5, which was still in the early prototype stage. In 1970, the daily production rate for the R6 was 900 and by 1971 the firm had manufactured 350,000. Over a million cars a year were now being produced by the Régie. This made Renault the third largest motor manufacturer in Europe. The figure represented an increase of 25% over that for 1968 and a record export figure of 530,000. It was 40% of France's automotive output and 45% of all car exports.

Le Car Mk I

The Renault Four was a small car with a small engine. It had four doors, rubber mats, and the sort of practicality that made it a sensible choice for the owners and workers of small farms and vineyards. Its aerodynamics were that of a large brick! Chic it wasn't. It was obvious that there were not going to be mega-powerful production Fours. The mechanicals would do, at least for the time being, but a new shape was required. The Renault 6 went some way towards providing it.

Enter in 1972, the Renault Five. The 845cc overhead valve engine and gearbox were retained, but the body was all new. The gear lever protruded through the dashboard as it did in its less fashionable older brother. The layout of the engine and gearbox, most unusual for a modern front drive car, has the gearbox sitting well to the front, underneath the radiator in fact, while the engine vies with the occupants of the front seats for their legroom! The position of the dashmounted gear lever was made necessary by the Heath Robinsonesque change rod which passed along the top of the engine and dropped straight down above the gearbox. Cars were soon offered with floor mounted gear levers!

Far more than just a car that slotted between the 4 and the 6, the 5 was in its own right a transportation unit of the new age – the epitome of the environmental motorcar. For the Régie it was gratifying that the new model almost immediately had conferred upon it the accolade of Car of the Year in the *Daily Telegraph*/BBC TV honours list. The car was winner of the low-price saloon category but was also voted overall runner-up to the Jaguar XJ 12.

The car's suspension was fully independent, with upper and lower wishbone arms, torsion bars, telescopic shock absorbers, and anti-roll bar at the front. The rear suspension comprised torsion bars, trailing arms, and telescopic shock absorbers. As more power was made available with the introduction of larger engines, a rear anti-roll bar was added. That quaint characteristic of small French cars was retained – the curious roll that convinces bystanders that the car was heading for imminent side body contact with the road. Indeed, some even went so far as to suggest that the side body mouldings were designed for just such occasions! They were,

The Renault Five has become a part of French life, like the Citroen 2CV and the Renault Four before it

in fact, a later addition, arriving with the TL model. From the outset, however, new materials were in evidence, in the shape of the moulded plastic front and rear bumpers.

The bumpers of the Renault 5 were trend setting, to say the least. Hardly any of today's cars have not adopted the same system. The use of glass-reinforced plastic was not new, but their use in quantity production was in its infancy, and following pioneer work in the United States, Renault adopted similar principles of mass production, but with improvements resulting from collaboration with a major French chemical company. It depended upon the use of pre-impregnated material (sheet moulding compound) made from glass fibre inpregnated with polyester resin. Cut-outs for the bumpers were put in giant presses at 150°C and accurately cured for final strength and contour. It was the first time in Europe that such units could be produced at the rate of 40 per hour.

The Five made its debut as a three door car, with 845cc engine. Over the years the model range grew. Five-door cars were introduced, and proved immensely popular, as did the automatic versions. The engine size was increased, firstly to 1108cc then to 1289cc and finally to 1397cc. It was to this last engine that a then novel, but now commonplace device was added, in the form of a Garrett type T3 turbocharger. With the help of a Weber 32 DIR 75 carburettor, a huge increase in torque and acceleration was achieved, with very modest demands on fuel consumption. The greatest change of all came in 1980, when the Dieppe factory made a batch of 1100 cars, all turbocharged, but with the engine moved from the front of the car to the back seat . . .

Above
*The unique engine/gearbox of the
Renault Four, showing the curious
linkage from dash-mounted lever to
gearbox at the front of the vehicle ...*

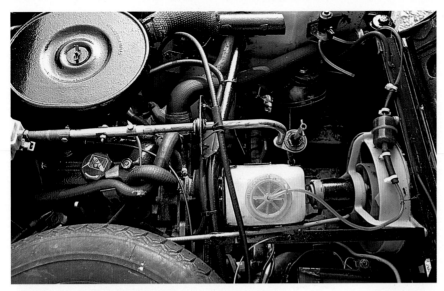

Left and below
*... and the same device (and
mechanicals) on an early Five*

*Designer Michel Boue did not live to
see his 'supermini' in production;
aimed at a more youthful market
than its predecessor, the Five soon
proved its worldwide appeal*

Described by Dreyfus as a car to go to church in, by the time the MkI was replaced in September 1984, more than 5.4 million had been built

Left

The little car was soon to be seen all over France, but it wasn't always built there. Several of Renault's 25 assembly plants around the world were soon working on the instant best-seller

Above

The Five was available first in three and then five door versions

The supermini was soon part of the backdrop to French life. The police bought thousands – but not all of them were marked ... The moulded bumpers were a real innovation, and would prove to be the blueprint for several other cars and manufacturers

The bumpers were glass-fibre
impregnated with polyester resin

Previous page and above
The MkI was a big hit across the
Channel almost from the outset

Opposite
The Five was a favourite option for
female drivers, but its appeal wasn't
limited to just one customer profile.
Larger engines were soon available –
956, 1289 and eventually Alpine-
tuned 1397 cc units. The plastic side
mouldings were another pioneering
use of such materials

*The car had a decided body-roll on
corners, dare one say a favourite
French design feature*

The cabin of a mid-1970s GTL

Above
The interior of the Turbo was sumptuous, with leather dashboard and steering wheel

Right
With the Dieppe-built mid-engined Turbo, Renault had undoubtedly turned the Five into a supercar

*Thick pile carpeting was everywhere,
even in the fairly cramped boot*

Above
*The bulbous lines half disguised an
increased rear track and enabled
massive air intakes to be sculpted in*

Right
*One unforeseen plus point of the new
version was that it retained the
marque's appeal for women, despite
the massive power increase*

The large Turbo badge on the rear was pretty redundant, because from any angle this was a car that promised performance, and speed in the supermini class almost always means turbocharging

*Strictly a two-seater, the Turbo was
the only rear-driven Five*

Mark II: Turbo Magic

Renault and the firm of Alpine in Dieppe, on the channel coast, have been collaborating for years. The speciality of the Alpine factory is developing and producing cars that can be rallied. With the mark I (front-drive) turbo, Alpine had increased the power of the 1397cc engine to 110bhp at 6000rpm, from a non-turboed 93bhp at 6400rpm. Both these Five Alpines were carburettor fed, and both were known as Renault Gordini in the United Kingdom, due to copyright problems with the name Alpine. (The Rootes group, later Chrysler had used the name on the Sunbeam Alpine, and the Five's contemporary Simca Alpine, later called Chrysler Alpine).

Examples of the Renault 5's sporting superiority had already been seen in the Monte Carlo Rally when, in 1978, mildly modified standard cars had scored second and third places, surprising everyone with the possibilities of front-wheel-drive, but in 1981 came the *tour de force* – an outright win in the same event by the R5 turbo, driven by French rally aces Jean Ragnotti and Jean-Marc Andrie.

Top place in the prestigious event was assured when Porsche challenger Jean-Luc Therier crashed on the first special stage over the fearsome Col de Turini in the final flat out battle of survivors over the French alps.

For Renault, the outstanding performance of the turbo in this gruelling event with its 2500 miles and 32 flat-out special stages, represented full justification for the company's intensive motor sport programme, not only in rallying but in formula events. The Monte Carlo victory provided a major boost to Renault sales worldwide, just after the firm had announced record production – 2,055,000 cars in 1980 – exports and turnover.

The rally presented the 5 Turbo with its toughest challenge up to that time: that of competing over snow and ice-bound mountains against the cream of Europe's works cars, including the customarily victorious Porsches and the new four-wheel-drive Audis. This was only the fourth event in which the turbo had competed, following trials in the previous year's Tour de France, Tour de Corse and Criterium des Cevennes.

The startling performance of the hot hatch more or less guaranteed entry into competition

By the mid 1980s, Renault had expanded their two-model range of the 1950s to include practically all categories of European car, from the utilitarian 4 (still being manufactured in 1987) to the V6 25 luxury saloon and Alpine GT Coupe. The lynchpin of this successful expansion was the Five in all its guises

Whilst motor sporting successes had an unquestionably beneficial effect on sales, the Renault 5 in any case continued to be sought after by all types of buyer and in all its varied forms. It was beating all records in France, where it had a penetration of 16% and a sales increase of 42% in 1980, compared with the previous year.

The 5 continued to notch up rally and circuit successes in the early 1980s, including 5th and 6th places in the 1982 Monte and 4th in the same event in 1984.

The Renault Elf 5 Turbo Cup championship started in Britain in April 1985 as part of a Europe-wide series for turbo saloon racing by Renault. The eleven-race series was strictly for the 125 mph Renault 5 GT Turbo 'Cup' version of the car produced in limited numbers for qualified drivers.

Mr Guy Bergeaud, then managing director of Renault UK, said: 'For Renault UK this new series marks an important milestone in our competition history. Not only is it important because we at Renault are totally commited to motor sport at all levels, but also because it provides us with an opportunity to underline this commitment by giving a cross-section of all drivers an opening in a new and exciting formula, so we are happy to be back in the sport in the UK in a positive and professional way.'

Meanwhile, for those with a keen interest in high performance on the road, there appeared in 1979 the Renault 5 Gordini, which has already been mentioned briefly. The Gordini designation provided a natural genetic link with the renowned 'sorcerer' Amédée Gordini, who made such epic contributions to Renault's success in motor sport, and who worked closely with Alpine at Dieppe. Out of Renault's UK target of 83,000 sales including 23,000 5s, the new model would account for 2,000. The Gordini was seen as a dual-role car – as a robust, practical family vehicle and young businessman's transport, whilst being also the perfect first car for drivers planning to take up motor sport.

Simultaneously, Renault introduced in Britain the model called 'Le Car', based on that which, under the same name, had achieved great success on the North American market and formed a major part of the Régie's deal with the American Motors Corporation. Technically, it shared the same mechanical components as the Renault 5 TS high-performance model, with 1300cc 64bhp motor.

Renault had come to the agreement with American Motors in January 1979. Originally it had been hoped to assemble the Renault 5 – Le Car – in the United States, but it proved not to be practicable, so the campaign was modified to provide for import and marketing as quickly as possible by a large network of AMC dealers in the US and Canada. By October, the liaison had strengthened considerably, the Régie's share in AMC's capital rising from an initial 5% to 22.5% and then 46%, with support from Renault Holding. 'Renault has become the fifth American automobile manufacturer' was a typical press comment.

By 1980, extraordinary things were happening at Dieppe! Alpine were giving birth to a Five with a difference. No longer front-driven, this odd

MkII Turbos differed from MkI in having leather upholstery and a nine-dial dashboard

car housed its engine behind the driver. Fuel injection replaced carburettors, and the wonder whine told you that there was a turbo on board. The car packed a punch, with 165bhp available, and it looked the part too! With massively flaired rear wheel arches housing huge air intakes, this car was not for the shy and retiring! Drivers often told how the car was raw, an animal to drive, and would sit shaking and creaking after a fast thrashing. Perhaps that was part of its appeal – for appeal it did, achieving a production run of 1362 units in mark I form. In 1982, the mark II arrived with alloy roof, doors, and tailgate, leather trim and seats, and a new, nine-dial dash.

In 1984 the Monster appeared. Called Maxi Five, it had no trace of the feminine lines that distinguished the normal Five. Using bits from other Renaults, (the 20/30 gearbox casing for example) and with a power output of a staggering 380–400bhp from its 1527cc turbocharged engine, the car enjoyed immediate rally success. The car looks like a cartoon caricature of itself, with enough lights at the front to drain the national grid.

The boot was just as cramped; the roof, doors and tailgate were now in alloy, not steel. The car continued to appeal to female owners everywhere

38

Charley Carcreff, veteran Five rallyer, works from Argenteuil, north-west of Paris. His business is called Automobiles Scora. In the yard are lines of MkI and MkII Turbos

Body shells, some showing the scars
of battle, litter the yard

The huge and unmistakeable air intakes appear almost to distort the body

Argenteuil was a favourite haunt of the Parisian-based Impressionist painters; what Monet would have done with the jumble of colours in Charley's workshop is anybody's guess. The Yacco lubricant sticker has been a familiar sign at French motor sport venues since the birth of road racing

Charley's Maxi Five – 'Le Monstre'. The number plate has been modified in order not to foul the airways in the front air dam. The aerofoil placed at the same level as the gutters helps to keep all that power on the ground; down-force is vital in a short-tailed vehicle like this

Above
The equally impressive cabin, fitted
out to M. Carcreff's rallying
requirements

Right
Le Monstre's heavy breather engine –
capable of 400bhp

Above
The chip in the wing reveals the intricate weave of Kevlar

Left
The body houses even bigger air intakes than on the standard Turbo

Supercinq

After thirteen years, the Five was showing its age. Still very front heavy, still roly-poly in the French manner. The replacement was to be a new car entirely – at least as new as one can get in the car industry, where series engines may have a life-span measured in decades. The new car had a new body and new running gear, in which torsion bars were replaced by MacPherson struts. Light alloy replaced cast iron in the gearbox, which was moved to a better weight distributing position underneath the engine. The new engine now sat East-West, instead of North-South, vastly improving passenger legroom, and making servicing easier. For the rest, the car was conventional, posing no serious problems mechanically.

The new body was cleverly styled – it looked like a Five – and yet? Smoother all round, the back lights were a stylistic tour de force. Renault were determined to keep the Five alive, but shunned the idea of a mark 2. The new car was simply Supercinq! Exploiting the desire to make an individual statement which the car offered from the outset, its UK advertising campaign used the slogan 'What's yours called?' Sales success continued; three- and five-door cars were offered with engine sizes from 956cc to 1721cc. The GTX 5 was fitted with a 1721cc engine, known as the 'motorway' engine because of its huge torque, and high speed cruising ability. A three-door 1397cc with turbocharger was also made. It was sold as the Turbo, not Alpine or Gordini, this being a purely Renault affair. The supercinq turbo was a huge improvement in refinement over the earlier car, although to label it 'refined' would be a mistake! It is, however, a 'mean machine' in the streetwise sense.

It established itself rapidly, and under Renault's benevolent hand a series of races was established as a truly pan-European tournament. The rules were strict, and had the useful marketing advantage of having only slightly modified production cars thundering around circuits such as Brands Hatch. The most obvious modification was the fitting of racing slick tyres, while under the bonnet the boost pressure was increased.

The Turbo also became the basis for a rather special little five, made in Belgium. Renault had been toying with the idea of producing a convertible five, the firm of EBS were asked to produce a feasibility study, and eventually, a prototype. Renault were extremely pleased with the outcome, but other factors intervened, and Renault abandoned the idea. EBS however, put to Renault the idea that they could build the convertible themselves, and production started in their Belgian factory in June 1987. The cars were imported through individual dealers, not by Renault themselves. Cars for the UK were distributed by Wimbledon

Above right
The style of the second generation retained the same kind of chic, but closer examination reveals that no body panels are replicated

Below right
The same then, only more so. Some abstruse Gallic advertising

Below far right
So fashionable had the Five become that the word was stuck on the bootlid, in English

47

dealers Radbourne Racing. EBS ceased production of the Five convertible in May 1991, after building a total of 1400, of which thirty were imported into the United Kingdom. Incidentally, not all convertibles were Turbos, although this was by far the most popular conversion. At least one base model five, known as the Campus, was the subject of a right-hand-drive convertible conversion.

With total production well over a million since its launch in October 1984, the R5, known universally as the Supercinq or Superfive, was the subject of a major revision for 1988, and there were numerous versions of the 3-door and 5-door cars with the choice of petrol, turbocharged and diesel motors. Daily production of the 5 had been running at a steady 2,000-plus for more than two years. By October 1985, a year after its launch, 500,000 had been built and a year later it had reached the 'magic million' milestone. It took 4.1% of the European market in 1986 (17 countries) and now aimed to consolidate its position in France and abroad through this widening of the range.

There were two new versions. The 5 GTX was a high-performance luxury-equipment model powered by a 90bhp 1.7-litre motor giving 115 mph top speed. It boasted remote-control central locking, tinted glass, 60/40 split rear seats and front fog lamps. The 5 Campus was the new base model with 1100 motor, trendy cloth upholstery and external side stripes, aimed at younger buyers and offering low running costs. Both new cars came in 3 or 5-door form.

Renault had earlier pioneered the availability of automatic transmission of cars of this modest size and there was a new version characterised by a system of numeric electronic control through a micro processor.

Engines ranged from the 1108cc 47bhp unit to the 1397cc turbo (now 120bhp) and the 1595cc 55bhp diesel. Two units were new to the 5 range – the 1237cc (from the Renault 9 and 11) and the 1721cc (from the 9, 11 and 21).

Above
Inevitably, various special editions were sold . . .

Right
. . . and use of the English word 'Five' continued

Above
*Supercinq has a more rounded,
sleeker look than the MkI, but the
design team had succeeded in that
most difficult of tasks: to make the
transition evolutionary, retaining the
feel of the earlier car*

The five door was a huge hit with families. Comparisons with, say, the Mini, were long since redundant. This was a car with a new level of refinement

Left
*Like the original Five, Supercinq
offered three or five doors*

Above
*The wheel at each corner design,
with very little body overhang, gave
maximum internal room and the
longest possible wheelbase for the
car's size*

Partly as a consequence of the four-square stance the ride was remarkably comfortable and the suspension was renowned for soaking up the bumps

Driving distances in France are of
course a scale up from those in the
UK. A trip from Paris to Nice in, say,
a 2CV was not a happy prospect, and
most of the old workhorses probably
lived and died close to the farm. The
Five, in contrast, can cover the
ground with the minimum of driver
fatigue

Images of the new France: stylish, functional and with a certain austerity. The second generation Five has not dated. The rear light cluster was a classically neat piece of design

Above
Even in Deauville, where style really counts, the Super five has presence

Left
It took just a year for 500,000 Supercinqs to be built and sold

Overleaf
This was supposed to be the classic 'car and deserted beach' shot; within minutes, company had arrived

Three door and five door posed on the Côte Fleurie. The Five was designed with go-anywhere utility in mind: though not, of course, in the Land Rover sense

There aren't many roads in the UK where parking is this easy. The proliferation of the superminis was an almost inevitable result of worsening congestion – and increasing expectations concerning vehicle refinement and performance

The Five is outside a grange where in
an earlier age animals were installed
for the winter. It's in the parking
space which would have been
reserved for the agricultural Deux-
Chevaux

The nationality of the Five was not emphasised as much at launch as it would be for the Clio. There are few people over the age of 25 in Britain who do not remember the clever approach that the advertisers took to the perennial marketeer's problem – how do you persuade a buyer that everyone wants your product, but it's also exclusive? One answer is to personalise it. The slogan was: 'Renault Five – what's yours called?'

A commercial van called Extra came
with various engine options including
diesel, and offered a large load space
with good economy, but style that
looked back to the Renault Four!

Supercinq Turbo; only available in three-door, this car was superbly well-equipped, and became de rigeur for the power-assisted man (or woman) about town

This 1989 Turbo belongs to an Osprey editor, so we had no choice but to include it. The earliest Supercinq Turbos did not have the rear 'winglet' – and they didn't like hotstarting. Fuel would vaporize in the carb with the engine switched off due to the heat generated by the turbo

Body colour wing mirrors . . .

*. . . and rear lights with that
pleasure-in-design that makes you
want to touch!*

Above
Inside, the car was stylish, had a good driving position, with bucket seats . . .

Right
. . . and a beautifully positioned and balanced gear lever

72

Left
A novel electronic key, which set the factory-fitted alarm and anti-theft system. Unless the electronic key was in place, the car could not be started

Below
Standard instrumentation, apart from, of course, the turbo gauge

Previous page
The five-spoke alloy wheels are standard on the phase 2 Supercinq Turbo only. Top-of-the-range Michelins fitted at the factory

Styling kits are available on the continent, as this car, shot in Italy, demonstrates

What the Five has always been superb at, and what the Turbo does superlatively, is to take you from here ...

. . . to there, with style! It's the lightness of the body that ensured the Turbo had the best 0–60 figures of all the hot hatches – 7.7 seconds

*Renault's Pan-European races
featured the Supercinq G.T. Turbo,
with very few real modifications ...*

Above
... a roll protection cage was fitted,
visible here behind the side door

Left
The engine is standard, but with a
strengthening brace and increased
turbo boost

Slick racing tyres and lots of advertising are the other necessary items

Steve Loughlan of Formula Print with his racing Turbo

Left
*Action at Castle Coombe sees cars lift
a wheel (or two!) on a tight bend*

Right
*Again, a braced but standard engine
gives credibility to the races*

Overleaf
*Owners and mechanics come from all
over the country to compete*

Above
The competition is intense, and the cars are of course pretty evenly matched

Right
The cost can be high, particularly if engines are blown, but relatively speaking, it is an inexpensive way to roar around a race track

Overleaf
Rallying the Five Turbo, Rallye d'Argentine, 1990. Note the radio link to base. Confidence in the integrity of the body is proved by this aggressive water splash. *(Photo courtesy Marzoli/Colorsport)*

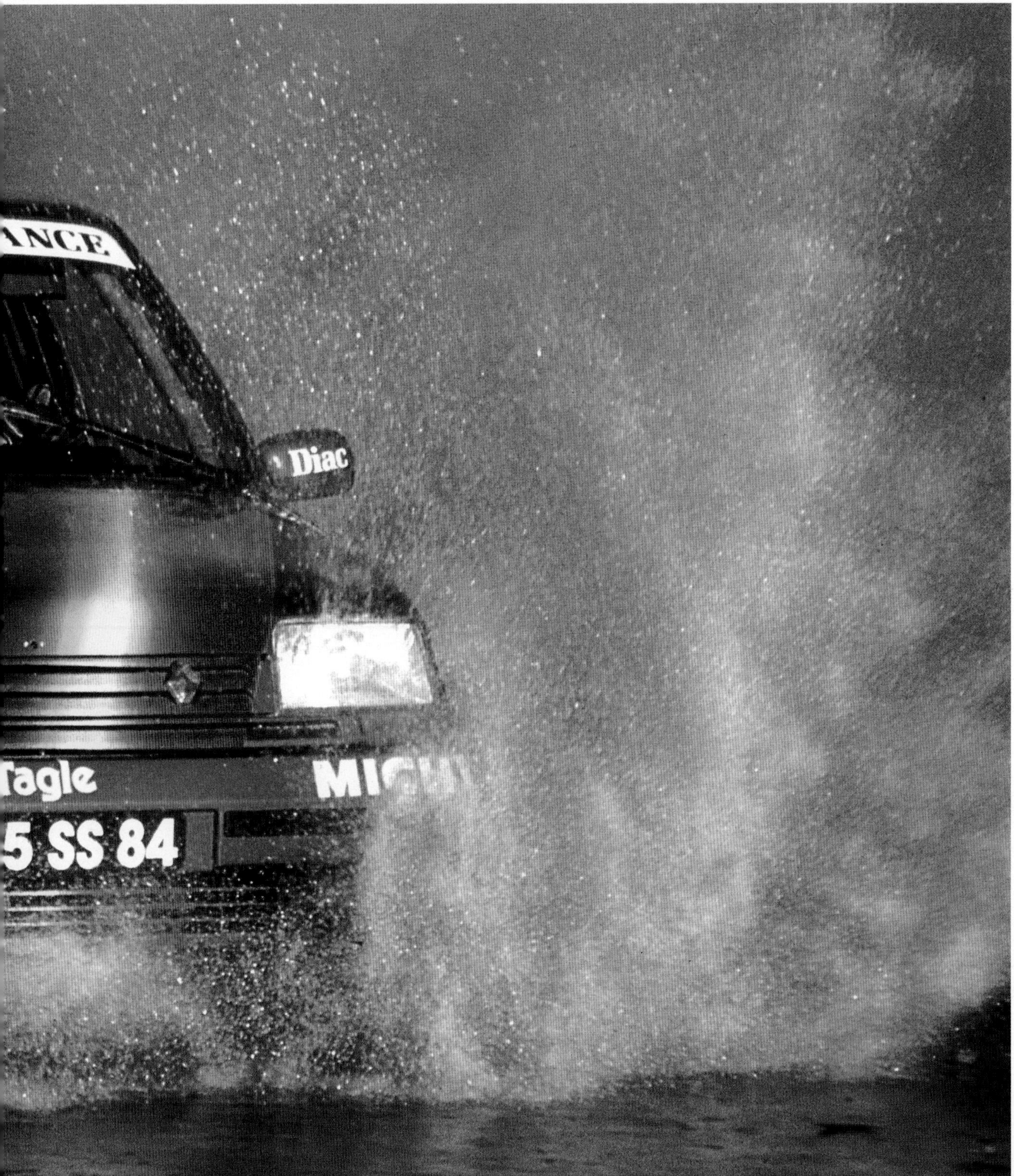

Renault Five GT Turbo, Rallye Sanremo, *October 1989; Alain Oreille with Gilles Thimonier were delighted Group N winners, despite a broken damper and a loose steering rack on the gravel stages.* (Photo P Huit/Colorsport)

Because the appeal of the Five was one of style, the problems of retaining that sense of balance in a soft top were immense. Hood down, most convertibles look better than their saloon counterparts ...

... but EBS of Belgium produced a design that looks good with the hood up as well

1400 were built, and only thirty were imported into the UK.

*Most conversions were based on the
G.T. Turbo, for obvious reasons*

Last of the Fives to be produced is called the Campus, indicating presumably that the frugal academic life need not be devoid of style

Against the imposing architecture of New Bedford College, Campus shows that it still has go-anywhere looks and has not been overtaken by '90s styling

Previous page
The comfortable interior of the basic Five shows that basic need not mean bare

Left
The lip on the hatch of the Five was quite high, a minor niggle which Renault's competitors were quick to take note of – and so did the French company when it came to the Clio

*Instruments exactly as you would
expect on a utility car, including all
that is really necessary*

The trusty and easily accessed engine, upgraded over the years from the days of the Renault Four

New Bedford College in Egham is
now part of the University of London.
It was founded by Thomas Holloway
as a college for the further education
of women. Work commenced in 1879;
the architect W.H. Crossland having
been asked to model the building on
the Château du Chambord in the
Loire Valley, using, instead of the
white stone of the Loire, red London
bricks. A suitable backdrop for a
truly European car

New Bedford College is now co-educational. The weighty Victorian interpretation of classical statuary decorates the grounds

Last chance to buy a new Five – 1992. Farewell to one of the most successful and well-loved cars ever built. Enter the next French superstar of the supermini class

Clio

The Paris motor show of 1988 was a particularly important occasion for Renault, for it saw the launch of their new middleweight, in the shape of the 19. With this new model came a series of important new engines, especially the Energy, a particularly economic and environmentally friendly four-pot. The Five was unable to take such units, and the launch of the new 19 had, in any case, marked a complete re-think at Renault. Much greater emphasis was being placed on build quality and paint finish. A renaissance was underway that would combine the swift surefootedness of the old Dieppe Alpines and the stance and beauty of the post-war Dauphines. The Five had made its mark, but it had also had its day. The end was in sight, and vast sums were spent developing the Five's replacement – the world's prettiest small car – The Clio.

First unveiled in June 1990, the Clio had new engines, gearboxes, a completely new interior, build quality like no other French small car, and a ride that leaves no doubt in the mind – this is a car built by people who know what they are doing. In the summer of 1991 the 16 valve 1764cc engined car came into the scene. It produces 137bhp at 6500rpm and is equipped with multipoint electronic injection coupled with electronic ignition. Its maximum speed is 130mph, and its level of interior specification and comfort is usually found in larger cars; the motoring press was unanimous – Renault had built a great small car.

The Clio is built at a rate of between 1500–1900 cars per day at the French plant at Flins; other countries are also building the cars – from Valladolid in Spain, Haven in Belgium and Setubal in Portugal. Farewell Five – welcome Clio. The Renault 5 is at the time of writing available in Campus form, being made alongside Clio at Flins, but it is gradually being phased out in favour of Clio, the European supermini.

Clio, in 16 valve guise, outside the Château de Chambord on which New Bedord College was modelled

The compact 1764cc 16 valve engine, first introduced in the summer of 1991. The Five could not have taken the new powerplant, even if Renault had wished to try

still cheaper to make. As time goes by, the economies of scale begin to favour Clio; and with the advent of the 16 valve Clio, Renault was able to replace the ageing Supercinq Turbo.

Certainly, in the words of Renault themselves 'Clio aims to build on the success of the Renault Five which has sold over 2.7 million units worldwide, with a model range that is as right for the current decade as the original Renault Five was appropriate for the 1970s at its announcement nearly 20 years ago.'

But Clio is a car that has taken on allcomers, and that compared with its class rivals, including Ford Fiesta, Rover Metro, Vauxhall Nova, Peugeot 205, Nissan Micra, VW Polo, Fiat Uno and Citroen AX, the Clio offered best interior space, and fuel-injection and catalytic conversion as standard on all petrol models.

Computer-aided design and engineering techniques were used extensively in the creation of the body. This allowed a reduction in the

number of separate parts – from 170 in the Renault 5 to 119 for Clio – to increase overall stiffness, sealing effectiveness and corrosion protection. Compared with the 5, steel thickness was increased in critical areas. High-strength low-alloy steel was used in key areas. Almost half the steel was pre-treated, including galvanised door and bonnet frames.

Significant dates in the design were:

Exterior design: Jan 1985, study begun and one-fifth scale models built. Oct 1985, full-scale models built. Apl 1986, four projects chosen. Sept 1986, project tests, design selected. May 1987, external design finalised.

Interior design: Apl 1985, study begun. July 1986, two projects selected and full-scale models built. Oct 1986, final project choice after test and development. Apl 1987, fascia design frozen. Oct 1987, complete interior design approved.

The Clio shows its superb lines; a bigger car than the Five, but still a light body, made possible by the use of computer-aided design and composite materials

Renault's Pan-European tournament has moved on to Clio, and Radbourne Racing were quick to produce a car to race

The inside of Radbourne's 16 valve
Clio; one bucket seat and a whole
host of safety modifications

Left
*Instrumentation on the racing Clio.
Right-hand-drive, and a lot of
strengthening in evidence*

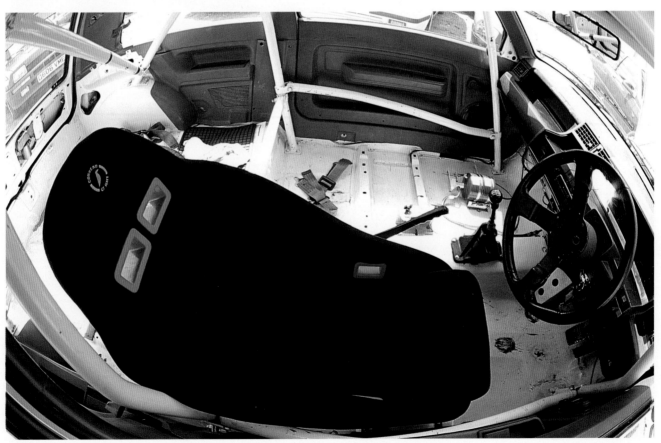

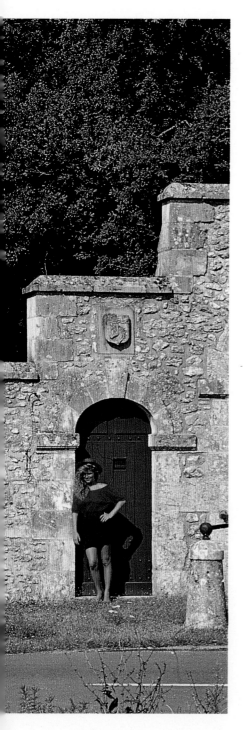

The differences between Five and Clio are so absolute that the only thing the two cars indisputably have in common is their market sector. But there must also be a lineage in terms of image-making and engineering knowledge for the supermini product, garnered from the success of the former to the advantage of the latter

Above
When the 16 valve Clio was launched in Britain, marketing used a line from an old pop song (covered by Ringo Starr): 'You're sixteen, you're beautiful and you're mine'. The same personalising approach that worked so dramatically well with the Five

Left

With no number, Five's replacement looks back to Renault's immediate post-war period, when names like Dauphine suited the pretty cars. The Clio isn't just built in France. The Spanish factory at Vallalolid also produces the car; thus continuing in the Renault supermini tradition. The plant was opened in 1952 and in 1974 produced its own four door 'notchback' version of the Five called the Siete, anticipating the parent company by some five years

*130mph from the 16 valves and a
level of interior specification that
puts some larger saloons to shame*